Poetic Pieces

Astrid Mychell

Poetic Pieces

§

Leading to Growth and

Understanding

ISBN-13: 978-1477605677

I dedicate this book to my mother Regina Hacker, my brother, Caleb and two sisters, Rockina and Joy. You all are my rock and you will always be.

<u>Contents</u>

Understanding

~*~*~

Letters to Myself

~*~*~

Lust, an Illusion of Love

~*~*~

Because First We are Human

~*~*~

Give Me the World and I'll Project its View Through My Eyes

~*~*~

God Is Love

~*~*~

~ Understanding~

A Lack of Understanding

I've been running,
For so long I feel as if the great winds have
Pierced my chest,
And the feet on which I stand have pulled a
Knife to my knees.
The swelling of my lungs suffocates my heart.
So I fall.

The heaving of my chest and the grinding of
My teeth
In the middle of this barren waste land,
Alone.
Face to face with me,
And my thoughts running free.

My eye leeks, one drop, then another.
One drop,
Two drops,
Five drops,

Too many to count.

Why do I weep?
God! I scream,
I can't find me!

The problem is I worry,
I worry until everything inside of me is in
This race,
Destination?
Break free.
I worry until tears fall from swollen eyes and
My insides lunge from my throat
And out my mouth.
Then I stop and have a conversation with the
Only one that really counts.

Dear God,
I know you know me so I won't explain,
But I do have a confession to make.

I am full of knowledge yet absent of
Understanding.
But I often wonder if my
Lack of understanding is the blame of a false
Knowledge.
What if the life we live is backwards
And our view of the abnormal is on the
Contrary?
What if the blind are the ones
That can really see
And we're the ones with the disability?
What if we're wrong in this belief that we
Should build more walls to house this never
Ending growing nation?
What if it were meant for us to build huts
Like the Africans do,
Using the gifts that you have given
Instead of taring them down for
Makeshift mansions.
What if we have it all wrong?
Get a good education so you can eat and
Supply your family with nice things.

Whatever happened to the
Enjoyment of learning?
It has become the sole means of survival.

I touch my chest only to raise a
Crimson hand.
Shot twice numbed once
Yet still alone in this barren waste land.
This I know, but I don't understand,
How I became the target.
But then isn't it a fact that life brings pain
And as we walk this road we're all in danger
Of being a bullets aim?
God said the farther my days stretch the
Greater my understanding.

Dirt beneath my seat as the sun pours its
Rays down upon me.
Clarity?
I think not, because I'm still trying to find
The difference between
Knowing and Understanding.

Intro

All nineteen of these poems that follow are a result of me growing and in the process understanding life. When I wrote *A Lack of Understanding* it was a direct representation of how I felt. There was so much I knew, or thought I knew, but very little that I truly understood, but then I hadn't really experienced anything. I look at myself now and I see the makings of a woman, no longer the remnants of a girl. I have realized that I don't have to understand everything, I just have to be willing to listen to the people that do. Life is full of surprises, full of mistakes, but most of all full of chances to learn. Every day I wake up I learn something new about myself, I see myself shedding the things I believed simply because that's what mom and dad taught me and forming my own opinions. I'm finding myself waking up with a smile and a prayer and my dreams becoming a reality. I've decided that I don't want to simply write stories with happy endings I want to be the main character in a story that ends well. And with all that I have learned I still have so much farther to go. In the mean time I found it only right to publish the pieces of me that have come together to form the work in progress that I am today.

~ Letters to Myself ~

Four Brands

These are my four brands on sex, drugs,
Drink and smoke.
These are my four brands
And how I got them

SEX,

Sex would lay with anyone that had an
Open space.
Sex was dicks open door
With no regrets or shame.
They came pounding and she laid there and
Took it all in
Because after all she gave consent.
Then at 12 sex made a baby in which she
Erased the name mommy from its lips
Because that was neither what she was
Nor desired to be.

Sex was nothing more than a wet open door
Inviting all in whether friend or foe.
Sex opened for the seeds that bloomed far
Too many but only six survived, minus one
Because he died.
Sex was a whore.
And see her sisters' laugh and joke because the
Past we can't change so we make it light to
Ease the pain.
Sex branded me with the fear of opening
Basement doors too early
So I vowed to keep nicked knees,
I didn't need no one to tell me because fear
Was screaming for me.
This is what Sex branded in me,
Unenjoyments possibility.

DRUGS

30 plus years of being caged,
Forget back hanging monkeys
30 plus years of needle pierced veins.

I probably couldn't even count all the holes
That you dug with that heroine laced shovel .
You stole then sold for money.
They placed you behind bars numerous
Times,
Fattened you up then threw you back to the
Wolves, where they came gnawing at your
Flesh leaving bone.
Unrecognizable.
I ran to my room and shed tears
What was left I wasn't even sure
I could call it you.
Scared straight
What ever happened to scared straight?
I wish you had been scared straight.
I mean haven't you seen enough of your kind
Resting six deep below your feet?
But then scared straight becomes
Nonexistent when fear left the picture a long
Time ago to repetition of the worst kind,
Habit.
It is my repetition to j-walk,

Fear slowly disappearing,
Habit.
Drugs branded in me the fear of dying
My promise long forgotten to the junkies and
Whores that became my definition.
A fear that this would be my eulogy.
A life with such promise lost with one shot
Clearly breaking my skin.
All my guests thanking God that I had died
Because at least in the grave I could no
Longer inflict myself with pain.
Drugs branded me with a fear so fiery red
I would scream kill me dead before I ever
Touch a needle to die
To the demon of addiction.

DRINK

Never thought you'd push your baby aside
Did you?
Never thought his childish joy would irritate
You did you?

But then you never thought that that one
Drink would control you.
Your father was an alcoholic then came you,
Your sons lookin' in the same direction and
He's only two.
Then you find a man that
Wobbles when he walks.
Intoxication is his perfume and the humor
You find in it all
Is his letter of approval.
I mean I just wish someone would crack the
Mold forget break it.
Drink branded in me not fear but disgust,
Disgust for what one sip of its lust filled cup
Could make me.
Dropping off that little you
Every Friday night
So you could kick it with
Your girls and get wasted.
When will you grow up and see that you just
Dropped off our future.

Drink branded in me disgust for
Unremembered nights and long prayers to a
Toilet seat.

SMOKE

Puff puff pass
But then you never passed
Puff puff...gasp.
Then let out a gut wrenching cough,
Spit mucus and snort.
Smoke.
Tobacco seeps from your pours,
You spray cologne as a cover
Sweet ashes are your scent.
Sending little ones running
Because you reek of decay
From the inside out.
Grayed hair, sunken eyes, no longer sexy
Though you try.
Smoke you are here for this second but the
Next you will be gone.

Puff puff...gasp

The enjoyment never lasts.

They say each day we die a little

You speeding up the process times ten,

Apparent in every wrinkle and

Misplaced fold.

Smoke you branded in me the fear

Of looking 60 at the age of 30

Along with all the complications

Your future may hold.

Smoke you branded in me the

Fear of getting old.

Suffocating on my deathbed from your firm

Grips hold.

Brands singed into the innermost parts of

My mind

I couldn't erase them if I tried.

And people ask me why this is what I choose

But wouldn't you do the same if someone

Had branded you?

These are my four brands on sex, drugs,

Drink and smoke.

These are my four brands,

And how I got them.

Strength, Courage, and Wisdom

India.Arie said it best
"Strength, Courage, and Wisdom its been
Inside me all along."
And yet I often find myself afraid to live.
Hiding in the shadows,
Singing in the chorus rather than
Taking the lead,
Sitting in the background and nodding
Instead of standing and speaking my piece.
But what can I say?
Rejection scares me.
Resulting in a mute me because
My voice is slowly losing its ability to speak.
But my ears hear the whispers.
"For God hath not given us the spirit of fear;
But of power, and of love,
And of a sound mind."
And if I only allowed it,

My strength would give me courage to

Showcase my wisdom.

A friend once told me

"Be assertive"

Summarizing my need to

Make my presence known

When I enter a room because, I'm somebody.

And until I show that off no one else will

Realize it.

See I can't keep putting off my confidence for

Tomorrow because each day past is one day

Closer to the day I miss my chance.

I want to paint,

I want to sing,

I want to dance.

All while people are watching.

Life is beautiful,

Mistakes and all.

And until I breathe in all possible outcomes.

Good and bad

Excepting them all,

I will never be able to

Embrace chance and step out on faith.

Because...

"Strength, Courage, and Wisdom

Has been inside me all along."

My Purest Form

Me in my purest form
Some might say is in my birthday suit
Revealing every inch of me,
But I beg to differ.

Me in my purest form
Is covered up yet still revealing everything.

It's not the make-up
That the world uses to define as beautiful
Or the whips and the kicks that are said to
Give us everything.
Yet instead it's the naps of my hair,
Perm all sweated out,
Because that is beauty.
It's the scars on my coat of ebony
Revealing my past, my history.

Me in my purest form
Is covered up yet still revealing everything.

It's the tears that roll down my cheeks.
My heart and soul poured out on a page.
Me in my purest form is the wind blowing on
My face,
Revealing all my impurities and
Imperfections Because yes,
I have many.
Thankful that if it weren't for the
Grace of God
That has purified and saved me.

Me in my purest form
Is covered up yet still revealing everything.

It's the bags that rest beneath my chinky eyes
After a long hard cry.
It's all the feelings that I've held inside.
Revealing themselves to the world because
It's not a sin

Me in my purest form
Is covered up yet still revealing everything.

Me in my purest form is allowing myself
To breath.

~Lust, an Illusion of Love~

One Love

Two minds forming one thought,
Two hearts having one beat,
Two souls becoming one flesh.

Marriage is an accumulation of these three
Allowing both man and woman
To happily be.
Through the hard times and the pain
Remembering that God still reigns.
Till death do you part you will forever be
Free of expression,
Giving and taking equally.
Forgiving faults,
Excepting strengths,
Loving each other for who you are,
Unconditionally.

Best friends and faithful lovers

Always remembering

That what God has put together

No man shall ever put asunder.

One Night Alone With You

It's crazy how much you can learn about

Yourself in a few moments.

I figured I would feel more,

Putting orgasm into quotes because that's

What people said virgins do.

But it wasn't like that at all,

See I was calm

Or as calm as one could be with gentle hands

Touching me.

And in that moment I understood the

Temptation that births babes before their

Time and....

Feeling the fullness of you

Against my backside

All I can remember thinking is

How do I get closer how do I go higher then

Wait...

Don't put your hand there because

I like it too much.
My back arched in tension until I realized I
Could relax in your arms.
I kept picturing the girl that is months along
And wondering if the father will be present.
I kept thinking of my opportunities and
My vow to never throw them away
For one good night.
And then I considered giving in because a
Part of me was dying to,
But there was no love there
Only lust accompanied
By your tongue on my neck.
Me saying shame on you to self because all I
Could think of was what else it could do.

It's crazy how much you can learn about
Yourself in a few moments.
I always felt it, now I know
Give me the chance to take someone in with
No fears or possible regrets
And I'll make fireworks.

I promise.

Like a baseball mashing into the catcher's

Glove, it hit me.

You hit me.

When I get the chance to give my all

I want to open wide

Scream loud and take everything in

And even though you gave me a good night

I'm not convinced you are the one

I'm meant to ride.

I just want to be honest with myself for once

In my life, raw.

If I would have turned over to face you,

If my lips would have touched yours

If I would have grabbed your manhood like I

Wanted to...

All hell would have broken loose.

It's easy to say I love you in a heated moment

But even easier to scream

I hate you when reality hits.

I don't know where we go from here

But I do know that at the moment I still feel
You on my lower back
At the top of my buttocks.
I do know that I still feel the heat of your
Tongue on my neck
And your hand trying to touch my breast,
But as good as it all felt and please know that
It felt good.
I can still feel me and the reality of the
Moments that followed
And I'm sorry but I refuse to give up my
Dreams for a few moments of
Your skilled hands
Well-endowed shaft and...
That mouth.

A Portrait of Love

That touch that gives me chills,

That look that tightens my thighs,

That whisper that lowers my lids,

That crown you place upon my head,

Those lips that quiet me.

That love that brings me to tears,

That ring you slid on with no fears.

A love jones of my own.

Voice caught in my throat

Because of every curve of every muscle.

That strength you exude that keeps me

Feeling...safe.

Sensual.

Sexual.

Intellectual.

That high that has me floating on cloud nine.

With no intention of ever coming down.

Being able to say,

That is mine.

Oozing with the definition of what we have

Come to be,

Of what others strive to be but fall short.

We are love.

With every touch,

With every kiss,

With every word...both unspoken and heard,

With every prayer,

With every silent and fulfilled fantasy.

WE. ARE. LOVE.

To Hold and Never Let Go

It was dark so I fell asleep.
That's when the dream came,

But I often prefer not to quote myself on it
Being a dream

Because it feels more like a memory.

"Can I hold you?"

A day late of the sharp pains shooting
Through my head

And an hour short of seeing the tears that
Caused these puffy eyes.

But none the less, he's here

Asking for hugs right when

I need it the most,

Though I wouldn't dare admit it.

But he didn't say hug did he?

His shirt as wet as if he had dove into a pool
Fully clothed.

I would call him a fool but it's my tears that
Wet him.

"Why did you say hold? You meant hug
Right?"

He planted love above my chin before
Answering.

I knew the answer then and I know it now.

When you hug you intend to let go

Sooner or later

But when you hold something it's because

You don't want to let it go,

Or my favorite,

It wouldn't be safe anywhere else.

I wish I could say that what followed was a
White horse and a multicolored sunset,

But it didn't.

Instead the moment after I knew I was in
Love, I pulled away.

I stepped back and took a good long look at
My sun kissed skin

And onyx locs.

When I closed my eyes I hadn't expected to
See him,

Short brown hair,

Pale white skin,

And a smile I could only imagine God having
Set aside just for me.

For a long while after that I told myself he
Was to...

Put together for someone like me.

I failed to see that he was exactly what I
Would need

To put myself back together.

He didn't mind getting dirty or the

Scrapes and bruises I regretfully gave.

He just held on

And when I was finally ready to hold on too

I found that all the pieces of me I had been
Searching for were with him.

It's light so I get up.

Each breath taken is slow and easy.

My own breathing took the same rhythm
Months ago.

No it wasn't a dream at all.

It was simply a memory of the making of my
Love poem.

~Because First We Are Human ~

Dark Skin Beauty

I am beautiful in my own right
And that happens to not include being light.
My hair isn't white girl strait,
Nor permed to look that way.
Instead it locks in everything that is me
I choose not to put on bronze face
Because it is simply reinvented black face.
Chocolate brown struggling to get
Recognition because there are
So few men mature enough to find my
Natural beauty,
Exotic.
"Black is Beautiful"... that's so cliché.
No Black is Sexy,
Black is Seductive
Black is Sensual
Black is Confidence
Black is Bold

Black Strong

Black is Real

Black is Me!!!

And you have the nerve to turn me down

Because I'm not the shade of hot mocha.

And you're right,

I am the color of the burning sun,

I am the color of a toasted almond

Honey I'm the color of true beauty.

Yet you finger me as angry

Because I hold my ground.

You assume I will put you down because

"That's what all Black women do."

But oh baby only if you knew.

I would cry with you,

I would stand with you,

I would ride or die with you.

I would *stay* with you.

But you will never know this because

You can't see past my deep brown skin tone.

Because on my face is written

"Loud, bitter, and angry
Approach at your own risk."
Causing tears to fall from my eyes because
What am I to tell
My dark sweet babies.
"Honey you came out black and because of
This, some, though not all
Will make assumptions about you and
Turn away,
But in the midst of it all I want you to know
That you are beautiful in our own right."
Leaving me fearing for the little girls that
Won't have mothers or fathers to tell them
The same.
"You are beautiful, so don't ever change."
Oh and how disgust and bile rise in my
Throat when a man has the nerve to say
He married light so his offspring would come
Out beautiful.
You face slapper you back stabber
You just indirectly called me and every other
Dark skin BEAUTY,

Ugly.

And for that I'm sorry but I hate you.

One day you woke up and came to the

Conclusion that we were

No longer good enough.

Light was better than dark

And white became like kryptonite.

But I refuse to let this faze me

Because I am beautiful in my own right.

And that happens to not include being light.

The Boy Inside

Eighteen years of bottled-up hurt.
Eighteen years of bottled-up pain.
Eighteen years of a broken young boy
Tugging on my shirt sleeve in an effort to
Receive a few minutes to speak his peace.
I pushed him away
In an effort to forget the past,
But there is no future without
An acceptance of the past.
So today I'm giving in.

Father you hurt me.
Not with what you did,
But with what you didn't do.
My hurt and pain turned into a fiery ball of
Anger straight from the pits of hell.
Grandma said don't hate.
But what am I to do
When your actions are deserving?
Who was I to look to?

Who was I to call?

Who was to be my definition of...

A MAN?

When people look at me they say they see

You, but when I look in the mirror

I see myself.

Broken.

Father did you love me?

Or did your love for me play second fiddle

To those children from your other family?

I grew into a man,

Hating men.

Couldn't keep a friend.

Is it because of you?

"Explain your relationship."

Well ma'am it was non-existent.

Last time I checked you can't get

Something from nothing.

How could I give when there was no take?...

Communication???

Tears fall but I wipe them aside.

I hate myself inside.

Why didn't your non-existing caring

Birth mine?

Eighteen years and everyday

I'm getting older.

And with each day that supposed love for

You grows colder.

If that little boy were father time

He would turn back the hands just for a

Minute alone with his father.

See he boasts hate

But I swear if you pulled back a layer you'd

Find pain

Because father,

You hurt me.

A Woman's Worth

I am worth more than the
Change in your pocket.
I am worth more than your twenties and
Ones stuck in my waist while I pop my gum.
I am worth more than your cheap side
Remarks regarding the thickness of my
Thighs and the rounding of my behind.
I am worth more than your overgrown sperm
Pierced into my womb and left to burn.
I am worth more,
Because I am the epitome of
Beauty and strength.
I am not to be toyed with or pushed around.
I find it funny;
You're surprised when I hold my ground.
I am mother, father, sister...
Lover, and still sane.
I demand respect because, I deserve it.

I am a shoulder,

I am a friend,

I am, *thee,* foundation.

A woman's worth?

Far more precious than rubies.

I am rare in my many shades,

And yet not that hard to find.

Disguised.

Because some days when you see me you will

Find that my mother didn't teach me

My worth.

So I act less than.

And then there are the days that

You will find

That my confidence is on high,

Because I know my worth.

And yet no matter which state you happen to

Find me,

I am still and will always be, worth more.

A woman's worth?

Just know it is far more than your nickels

And dimes, and half-hearted tries.

Trust Issues

Teach me.
Teach my heart to beat with the same
Rhythm as your own
Because mine seems to have fallen off tempo.
I'm singing every note but the right one,
Tuning you out because that's what my
Father taught me.
Singing along to silence
Trying to keep the beat
How can you harmonize
With what's not there?
It takes two to be in harmony so the fact that
I'm singing solo makes no sense.

Oh the things we'll do for a nice smile and a
Sweet disposition,

It's time we pick up those glasses that give us
X-ray vision to see through those honey
Dipped words,
And zero in on the intentions.

Oh the things we do for love.
No, oh the things we do for like.

Deception written in your eyes laced on your
Lips and yet I have become like Helen Keller
Both deaf and blind.
And I swore that I was the smart one
Because she fell for saggy pants, a staggered
Walk, funky talk and two little ones resting
In back pockets waiting to pop out
Unannounced followed by…
"Oh, did I forget to mention that?"

But see I found,
I FOUND,
Myself a corporate man

With pants that fit his waste, and stride that
Boasted confidence,
And I was confident that he was the one.
Not the one that would love and cherish me
But the one that would give me stability.

Oh the things we do for love.
No, oh the things we do for like.

Soft kisses like the poison of Snow's apple
He placed a noose around my neck and hung
Me with his sweet tasting words,
Telling me of all the things he planned to do
But in truth...
He had no intention of following though.
A man of his word,
He was everything but.
And I swore that I was the smart one,
But now we both look dumb
And when I finally loosed myself I bounced
Around like Ali

Promising to float like a butterfly before I let
Him weigh me,

But in some cases scares weigh more than
Bricks because you can't feel them.
Then one day someone came along and
Shoved my trust issues in my face.
They say you are what you eat and
I find myself daily snacking on doubt.

So teach me.
Teach my heart to beat with the same
Rhythm of your own
Because mine seems to have fallen off tempo.
I'm singing every note but the right one
Tuning you out because that's what my
Father taught me.
Singing along to silence
Trying to keep the beat
How can you harmonize
With what's not there?

It takes two to be in harmony so the fact that

I'm singing solo makes no sense

And I didn't realize that I was so low until

The weight of my doubt

Manifested in pounds.

I thought about shoving a finger toward my

Belly producing an upchuck of these

Damaging effects

But a quick fix only leads to

A quick destruction,

So until I am given a proper discharge from

This demon

Teach me.

Teach my heart to beat with the same

Rhythm of your own.

~Give Me the World and I'll Project its View

Through My Eyes~

Common Sense

They said we lacked understanding.
But what they didn't know then and still
Don't know now,
Is that we had common sense.
The common sense that
Dwindled away sometime after adolescence
And became what a young woman's mother
Began to say.
"Common sense ain't common to everyone."
But it is common sense for a five year old
Boy to hate the phrase "Black People"
Because when he looks in the mirror
He sees, brown.
Or for the child with multiple scrapes
On her knee because of all the times
She has tried
Without needing the phrase,
"If at first you don't succeed...."

This is the common sense

They were born with,

We were born with.

But somewhere down the road

Our knees began to ache from growth

And our bodies changed and we were no

Longer cute enough

For the old ladies in white gloves that

Showed us to our Sunday seats,

To pinch our cheeks.

We started paying closer attention to the

Opinions of those around us

Which led to a questioning of self that

Tampered with our,

Common sense.

We lost ourselves and were frightened

Because though we used the phrase

We no longer knew what was common sense

But what was rather,

Common.

Scared though as a child it was common

Sense to be fearless,

Hating though as a child it was common
Sense to love,
Giving up though as a child it was common
Sense to pull through and dry the tears of
Those that shed them.
We were strong,
And became weak
Because we lost the common sense of faith.
"The substance of things hoped for,
The evidence of things not seen."
It's the common sense that tells us that such
A beautiful and complex people couldn't
Have just come about by accident.
The common sense that holds
Our backs up straight because
We are strong, and we are powerful
And we are like none other.
And yet every day someone has to be
Reminded of this.
Our youthful common sense trapped in the
Crevices of our mind

Infected by doubt and conformity that can
Only be cured by the common sensibility of
Freed self.
To cease the fact that every day brings the
Loss of one's precious,
God given,
Common sense.

The Rich

The rich are getting richer and the poor are
Dying off.
Hey I'm an ex abuser...
Every month the government signs a check
To write them off.
More money for the dealers.
More business for the morgue.
And oh the mirror of a child's eyes
Showing the consequences of your actions
But instead of making change you look away.
It doesn't make it go away.
I often wonder,
What makes a man?
The struggle of his youth or
The results they birth within that shine
Through.

It's a business.

Divide and conquer.

Grab the two men at the bottom of the pole

Show them that they're different

And one should demand respect.

Turn them against each other

Because together they can conquer,

Together they'll defeat.

And we can't have that.

Besides, the ones at the top have their own

Problems to tend too,

Trying to kill each other off

So one can stand alone.

News flash, one can't stand alone.

Oh the smell of greed.

It reeks of dirty hands,

Undercover operations

And the blood of those stepped on

To get to the top.

"Life's not fair."

Man that's bull,

Shhhh I don't want to hear it.

With enough money to go around

Yet we find comfort in uneven distribution.
The rich are getting richer
And poor are dying off.

It's not a business it's a war
In which sometimes I feel I've lost.
If I had a nickel for every dime I was
Required to pay
To build those million dollar houses in which
I will never stay.

The senators done gone and stole my taxes
Cashed them in as down payments...
Mr. Man,
I know you've got your platinum and I know
You've got your gold
But I've got little children
That at night get really cold.
Would you give a room in your mansion?
Your pocket full of change?
Pay my bill that's overdue?

I work hard for my pennies could I say the
Same for you?
The rich are getting richer
And the poor are dying off.

Blind Privilege

The rain falls clouding our vision,
Giving the illusion that privilege is worldwide
When really it's blind.
Constantly reminded of the
Devastation overseas
But, what of the devastation
In front of our faces.
Death rowed streets lined with single parent
Families and the places filled with
Racist faces,
Killing by character assassination.
Our neighbors in D.C. rarely leaving our
Eleven o'clock news slots free,
With word of yet another killing.
Housing drug infusion that birth illusions
Leaving us accustomed to the wrong we see.
Abuse only recognized on TV
Rappers admitting they'd rather ditch

Than snitch on the wrong they see.

Daily.

We fly blind.

Noses held so high when in reality we stand

Eye to eye.

What if our mission was the subtraction of

False satisfaction?

All that glitters ain't gold

And money gets old.

We are steady trying to knock each other

Down when we ourselves are on the ground.

Having the nerve to proclaim,

Can't make it without a college degree in the

Twenty-first century,

Never minding the young ones

That grow up in the slums

And even some in my neighborhood that just

Don't have the funds.

And before you go sayin' it's because money

Doesn't get around

Let me tell you, Oh it gets around,

It just very rarely gets...*Down*

If only we'd take off our blinders long enough
To see that privilege doesn't belong
To everybody.
Maybe if I didn't have such nice things that
Homeless guy could eat and if we all reached
Out a hand encouraging each other to believe
We wouldn't have so many
Bums on the street.
But instead we're left with this privilege
Made wall separating what is to be believed,
The less from the more.
If only we would allow our minds eye to see,
All that separates us are things and in
Actuality our equality should lie in the fact
That we're all human beings,
Enslaved by this belief that privilege allows
Us to see the status of each
When really,
It's blinding.

Life's Mascaraed Ball

I was invited to a mascaraed ball
So I wore my smile.
Red lips white teeth, no one recognized me.
I won best disguise.
After twelve hours of waiting for the clock to
Chime at the top of the hour rather than
Losing my glass slippers and disguise,
Life took rocks and stoned me.
Life took knives and cut me.
Life shot me with the same bullets it had
Used on everyone else
So I smiled like everyone else.
High cheeks burning muscles, it hurt.
So I closed my eyes...

Long train rides two seats on my left side a
Young black man smiles,
So hard that laughter falls from his lips,

I wonder what caused it.

Unsubtle outburst, I recognize him.

He was at the mascaraed ball too

And seeing it is tugging on my hearts strings

But masks are pulling on his life's strings.

Puppets, masks, it reminds me of Pinocchio

But instead of longing to be a real boy this

Rotted woods only goal is to make it through

Life without being discovered,

Without masks being uncovered...

To rot a wood stump quick you bore holes in it

Leavings open entrances for

Decaying antibodies

Breaking down the man,

Breaking down the hu-man.

The decayed holes are unsightly,

People point and look, it's frightening.

We need a cover-up...

You have been cordially invited to
Life's Mascaraed Ball

Being held on every street corner in every
Home along with every public and private
Place, starting at birth for some and at the
First sign of unbearable pain for others.
Hope to see you there!

No whistles, no bells
Nothing to draw too much attention
We show up at our appointed times with
Bright multicolored smiles
Everyone whispering about who is who.
The decay is tucked away inside.
We did it, we found a way to hide the ugly
But don't worry decay isn't only looks,
It stinks too.
Sorry to burst a bubble but smiles can't hide
Everything.

My eyes pried open, see
This is your life
This is my life
This is our life

Never thought you'd wish for party crashers
Did you?
And when the music fades and I find myself
Staring into the eyes of my partners
I have to ask myself,
Was it all a dream,
Or the remembrance of a possibility?

~God Is Love~

High

So I do this thing where I close my eyes,
And imagine myself atop a mountain.
Overlooking rivers, and valleys and seas.
Things that I can only see when I am,
High.
Now I'm not talking about that high you get
From injecting and sniffing toxins and trees
That will eventually destroy me.
No this is a spiritual high
Where Jesus injects me with peace and I
Snort faith.
See this high unlike most forces me into
The rain and to experience pain.
With this high instead of being forced from
My body to hover in some euphoric state,
I'm locked inside this brown skin cage of
Mine forced to realize that I am human,
Inhabiting every wicked way in me.

There's no, "over my dead body" escape

By way of dirty needles or a missed vain.

I know it sounds insane

But this is the only way that

God and I can relate.

This high is me seeing me for all of me,

Which is nothing

Needing God if I plan to face a darkened

World full of drug highs and suicides.

Now you must agree we need a light.

That's why God gave me these words offering

An entrance to this,

Spiritual height.

Grace and Mercy

I am unlovable,
Yes you are and that is why I love you.
I am unforgivable,
Yes you are and that is why I forgive you.
I deserve to rot in hell,
Yes you do and that is why I give you heaven.

The scum of the ground was how I was found
I saw him walking when he started talking as
If we were the same.
I begged him to leave but he fell to his knees
And said he wanted me
I said I was fine which of course was a lie.
He saw it in my eyes.
He said come unto me and
You shall be clean.
I looked at a bruised and battered me,
Yet refused to admit my shortcomings.

He stretched out a hand and
Proceeded to stand.

I am unlovable,
Yes you are and that is why I love you.
I am unforgivable,
Yes you are and that is why I forgive you.
I deserve to rot in hell,
Yes you do and that is why I give you heaven.

How could I believe the things he said to me?
He walked away as expected,
But to a hill where he cut down a tree and
Said it was for me.
He carved out a cross just before my sins
Came upon him.
He didn't fidget or fight
He just let them fall on him.
They nailed down his hands
And then his feet.
That cold dark night Jesus died for me.
I cried for he hadn't lied

Three days later as my head rested in my lap
I felt a hand on my back

Come unto me and you shall be clean.
He reached for my hand
And helped me to stand
He had died for me and rose for me
How could I resist such a loving man
I walked away that day cleansed and new
For Jesus had saved me
Just like he said he would do.

Kneeling Naked

I once read a story about a girl that

Fell to her knees

Pressed her face to the floor

And raised her backside to the ceiling.

When I first read this I was

Embarrassed for her,

In front of all those people...exposed.

But what I failed to realize is that she

Wasn't exposed in front of all those people,

She was exposed in front of God.

There's something about being laid out at
Jesus' feet.

I think it's because when we are at Gods feet

We are right where we are supposed to be.

Kneeling naked

Exposed and yet warm from the embrace of God's love.

And that's when everyone else fades away.

My Prayer

God.
Some days my feet burn
From pushing forward when
I have nothing left.
Carry me.
God.
Some days I'm so confident that I know
Where I'm going,
That is until I find myself lost.
Guide me.
God.
Some days I cry out in frustration
From the lack of my better half.
Love me.
And then there are those days when I am so
Beat down that
I bang on these walls of flesh and bone but
Am too weak to get out.

Free me.

I can do nothing alone, I need you.

So my prayer for today and forever

Is that you would go before me to

Clear my path.

Go behind me to catch me if I fall

And walk beside me to hold my hand.

So that when the rain falls

When the lightning strikes

When the thunder booms

And when my fears outweigh my faith

I will know that I can make it

I will know that I can pull through

Because nothing I will ever do will ever be

Done alone.

Acknowledgements

How can I in my ignorance, regarding any particular subject matter, find myself puffed up enough to say that this was all me? I am but a lowly body that by some has been seen as more, and therefore have become someone that will one day be deemed as great. I would like to start by thanking my mother. Not only for the simple fact that if it were not by way of her I would not be, but also for every day I saw her rise from the struggles of life with a smile on her face and a prayer on her lips. Mama I thank you.

Secondly, I would like to thank my aunt Kyra Hicks, which to be precise is my cousin but some people touch your life in such a way that their actual title becomes insignificant because they are so much more. Without her this book would have in no way been possible. Her belief in me planted a belief in myself, and for that I thank her.

Then there is the group of poets that took me in and showed me that poetry was not simply a hobby, but a way of life. Well Versed Xpressions, a writing organization at the University of North Carolina at Greensboro, sharpened the edges of my craft and reintroduced me to the reason I began writing in the first place.

Lastly, I would like to thank God. Placed last because I have found that it is often the things we close with that resonate the most. Without God there would be no writing for me because there would be no talent. Some days when I put pen to paper I find myself baffled because of the things I am able to visualize though I have not personally experienced them. I like to think of myself as the product of a blessing undeserved. And for that I am thankful.

About the Author

Astrid Mychell Hacker was born and raised in Alexandria, Virginia. Upon graduating she moved to Greensboro, North Carolina to further her education at the University of North Carolina at Greensboro where she currently studies. She has other spoken word pieces featured on the album "Waking up" by Caleb. This is her first published work, the beginning of much more to come as she is an aspiring author and poet.

16619366R00058

Made in the USA
Lexington, KY
02 August 2012